Witness to Gaza
Poetry of Struggle and Solidarity

First published in the UK by Beacon Books and Media Ltd
Earl Business Centre, Dowry Street, Oldham OL8 2PF UK.

Copyright © Fadoua Govaerts 2025

The right of Fadoua Govaerts to be identified as the author of this work has been asserted in accordance with the Copyright, Designs and Patents Act 1988. All rights reserved. This book may not be reproduced, scanned, transmitted or distributed in any printed or electronic form or by any means without the prior written permission from the copyright owners, except in the case of brief quotations embedded in critical reviews and other non-commercial uses permitted by copyright law.

Cover art © 2025 Laila Kassab. All rights reserved by the artist. Used under license.

First edition published in 2025

www.beaconbooks.net

ISBN	978-1-916955-59-2	Paperback
ISBN	978-1-916955-60-8	Ebook

Cataloging-in-Publication record for this book is available from the British Library

Witness to Gaza
Poetry of Struggle and Solidarity

Anthology edited by
Dr. Fadoua Govaerts

Dedication

This collection of poetry is dedicated to the lives lost and the resilience of those who have survived in Gaza. May it stand as both a tribute and a message: we bear witness, and we will not forget nor forgive until justice prevails and they live in peace.

Contents

Acknowledgements ix
Introduction 1
I wander lonely as a star 3
    Lubna Ahmad Abu Dahrouj, Gaza, Palestine
I survive to die 4
    Lubna Ahmad Abu Dahrouj, Gaza, Palestine
Let's leave! 6
    Dr. Ali Tawil, Gaza, Palestine
Palestine, My Palestine 7
    Raaya Elzamzamy, USA
Lost Child 8
    Bibi Ashia Akhtar
Why Why Why 9
    Aria-Rose Harper (age 9)
Palestine Palestine 10
    Aria-Rose Harper (age 9)
My Gaza Dream 12
    Hiba Anwer Moten
The Silence of Law 13
    Major Hidayat Muhamad, Malaysian Army
Tents 15
    Repi Begum
Remorse of a witness 16
    Ayse Meryem, Istanbul, Turkiye
O Dear World 18
    Shifa Mohammad Munshi
Palestine: Our Strawberry Farm 20
    Dr Shrehan Lynch, London, UK
Boundaries of Longing 21
    Fatena Abu Mostafa, Gaza, Palestine
Unreachable North, Unbreakable Bonds 24
    Fatena Abu Mostafa, Gaza, Palestine
Never ask me again 26
    Fatena Abu Mostafa, Gaza, Palestine
It is not easy lifting the souls of Gaza 28
    Fadoua Govaerts
The Guilt of Motherhood 30
    Dr Fadoua Govaerts

The Keffiyeh in the Crowd 32
    Dr Fadoua Govaerts
As the sun comes up ? 34
    Francesca Vowles, Trowbridge UK)
And Samson Wept – Eyeless in Gaza 35
    Bryn Jones, Bath, UK
I am Gaza. 36
    Asiya Ali (13) UK
I wonder 38
    Asiya Ali (13) UK
In our eyes 41
    Asiya Ali (13) UK
Cry Gaza 43
    Beas Bhattacharya, Bath, UK
One blood, one Freedom 45
    Beas Bhattacharya, Bath, UK
A Morning like No Other, ... 47
    Johnny T Fox , Swindon, UK
THE GREAT RETURN 49
    Ira Khalid
335 Bullets 335 51
    Tony Hillier, Swindon, UK
on catastrophe 53
    Memoona Ahmed, Oxford, UK
Winter Hill 56
    D.R.Sweeney Wiltshire, UK.
Weep for the Little Children 57
    D.R.Sweeney Wiltshire, UK.
Olive Tree 59
    Emily Masi-Cacchio
Poor Palestine 60
    Lola Ali (age 7)
Baby Boy 61
    Orlaith O'Neill, Wiltshire
Daddy's girl 62
    Orlaith O'Neill (Wiltshire)
How? 63
    Orlaith O'Neill (Wiltshire)
Raging Love 64
    Orlaith O'Neill (Wiltshire)

The recycling of Palestinians 66
    Orlaith O'Neill (Wiltshire)
Shaban al-Dalou 67
    Orlaith O'Neill (Wiltshire)
The Terrorist of Bil'in 68
    Orlaith O'Neill (Wiltshire)
This our story 69
    Mindy V
The Sun – For Empathy 71
    Sol Shalaby Bath, UK
Oranges 72
    Sol Shalaby Bath, UK
Gaza 73
    Moran Hajyahya, 20
I am from Gaza 75
    Ibrahim Massri, Gaza, Palestine
Please Free Palestine 77
    Zoraiz Fahad Syed, Swindon, UK, aged 8
Centre 78
    Paul Menard
From the Hearts of Palestine 79
    Michelle Amani Darhali
A Child of Palestine 80
    Michelle Amani Darhali
The Price of War 81
    Michelle Amani Darhali
A Child of War 82
    Michelle Amani Darhali
A human Refugee 83
    Michelle Amani Darhali
Whispers of Tomorrow 84
    Sidra Mobeen, Swindon, UK
Paradise 86
    Khadija Rouf
Pomegranate 87
    Khadija Rouf
The Twelve Days of Christmas In Gaza 89
    Jane Samson
    Adapted version of this carol read out at the Avon Pension Fund
    Committee meeting in Keynsham, UK

The Fall of Gaza..93
    Stella Mortazavi
Until...94
    Stella Mortazavi

Acknowledgements

This book would not have been possible without the contributors of this book, the humans standing in solidarity, responding to the call to create this work. I extend my gratitude to all the contributors who courageously shared the heavy emotional burdens they carry, putting them into words to share with the world. This includes the artist Laila Kassab, who kindly gave us permission to use her artwork, *Melody of Freedom*. She adds, "In the bombed city, an old bird curses its very survival. Mary searches for anti-war poems and finds a bird singing a tune of freedom."

Special thanks go to all members of Swindon Palestine Solidarity coming out regardless of the British weather, especially the young children in Swindon. They inspired this work, when taking to the streets in protest and brought their poems as a heartfelt expression of their emotions. They give us hope, that the Palestinian cause will not rest, until they are free.

I am particularly grateful to the authors from Gaza featured in this collection. Through the reach of social media, they learned about our call for poetry submissions. While they were touched by the initiative, the truth is, I was deeply moved by their effort to contribute. Their poems, filled with raw emotions of grief, pain, and steadfastness, are a testament to their unyielding spirit.

Finally, I would like to thank the publishers and editors at Beacon Books. When approached with this idea, they did not hesitate. Instead, they embraced the opportunity, seizing the moment to make this book a reality.

Introduction

This collection brings together a tapestry of raw voices from Swindon, across the UK, and around the world, including Gaza itself. Each poem is a poignant expression of emotions stirred by witnessing the unimaginable: a people enduring profound suffering, loss, and resilience. The inspiration for this anthology began with children as young as six, at a protest, standing on a stage in cold, wet British weather, sharing their fears, anger, pain, and grief with local crowds. These children, through conversations with their families, grappled with words they should not even be old enough to understand—*genocide, apartheid, occupation, imperialism, Zionism*. Yet, they not only understood but articulated their feelings with such clarity and truth that often eludes adults. Their unfiltered, fearless expressions cut to the core, reminding us of the power of honest language—language that we, as adults, sometimes lose.

In a town like Swindon, on our usual spot in Regent Circus, one young poet followed another, often leaving protesters in tears and giving fellow protesters hugs in that moment. Adults shared their verses too, often inspired by the courage of these children. I felt an overwhelming sense of responsibility to ensure these voices were not lost. These poems needed to be preserved, recited, and passed on—a legacy for future generations when our present becomes history. This collection documents how we, far away in Swindon, felt and how we coped with witnessing the unbearable, alongside sharing our frustrations on our marches through our Town Centre.

Because not all poems were saved after our protests, Swindon Palestine Solidarity announced the call for poems in our local events and shared the initiative to collate the poems online. As a result, the contributors, ranging from children to adults, from seasoned poets to first-time writers, have poured their hearts into these verses. Through the power of social media, the poems reached from the streets of Swindon to the shores of Gaza, each with words resonate with grief, hope, togetherness and unwavering solidarity.

The poems from Gaza hold a unique place in this collection. They are written amidst the harrowing realities they describe, offering raw, unfiltered glimpses into lives lived under a sky lit by rockets and drones. These voices, despite unimaginable adversity, find a way to rise, echoing their steadfastness and humanity, a testament to the resilience of a people who continue to rise against unimaginable adversity. Including their voices is both an honour and a solemn responsibility. Hopefully, this collection does justice to their courage and serves as a message of hope and warmth—that they are not alone. Despite our distance, and limitations, we have tried, we will continue to try, in our own unique ways to stop this genocide.

This anthology is not just a collection of poetry; it is a call to action. It is a reminder that silence is just not an option if we are to honour our shared humanity and strive for a world of peace, dignity, and justice. It is a testament to the power of words to connect, to heal, and to bear witness. It transcends borders, uniting us in the shared acknowledgment of injustice and the universal yearning for peace and dignity. Putting these poems together needed a lot of courage and energy, as if reading the mind of each individual, opening their souls and hearts. I am sure as you read one after another, you'll go through a similar journey; ranging from hope to despair, pain and anger. I hope these poems serve as a reminder of our shared humanity and a call to action to strive for a world where every voice is heard, every life is valued, and freedom from occupation and the torture of any people is a reality.

In Solidarity, Justice and Peace
Dr Fadoua Govaerts
Secretary Swindon Palestine Solidarity

I wander lonely as a star

I wander lonely as a star.
Over Gaza sky, where loud silence settles down,
Where Gazans weep and gasp for breath.
I wander lonely as a star.
Over Gaza sky, where bodies tumble in the open,
And sometimes, if they're lucky, buried in the silence of graves.
I wander lonely as a star,
Over Gaza sky, where children sleep with empty stomachs.
And tonight, no "once upon a time" is told,
For stories vanished with their mothers' murmurs.
I wander lonely as a star,
Over Gaza sky, where the wind, though soft,
Carries the dust of rubble, the remains of flesh,
And the sound of stifled ughs.
I wander lonely as a star,
Over Gaza sky,
Where peace at dawn is lost,
And souls are targeted in the worshippers' ranks.
The stubborn, angry waves strike the shore,
Yet never break free.
And I ask: have you seen a star falling down?
And when it falls, does it simply burn?
And does its burning light mark a spark in the genuine hearts?

Lubna Ahmad Abu Dahrouj, Gaza, Palestine

I survive to die

Despite your concentrated efforts to end me,

I have survived, randomly.

I have returned to the rubble that once was my home.

have rolled up my sleeves like you roll the dice of death

and have pitched a small tent.

Despite bloodshed on all sides,

despite the scent of death trapped in my nostrils,

despite the buzzing of your circling drones,

despite painful memories of losses past, I read my book, feed the kitties, have a cup of coffee,

prepare something to eat.

No sooner do take the first bite than your bullet hits me, unexpected as a hidden hand.

aga poets sweety

I wish you had given me a minute to brace myself for my untimely exit, to play my best cards, or at least to chew my food.
Upon my sudden death, they photograph my corpse to show

those who cared that died with food stuck in my mouth, that was still trying, still playing. My demise is a recurring theme in an impossible game.

I died today.

Others will die tomorrow.

Every day, we wait for Godot.

Every day, we survive to die.

And every day,

they keep rolling their dice.

Lubna Ahmad Abu Dahrouj, Gaza, Palestine

Note: This poem was published online through Gaza Poets Society

Let's leave!

Let's leave from here to there,
to the other tent or to the other hell,
but;
will the road be safe,
I wonder,
or will the specter of death catch us
shortly before the end?
Wandering aimlessly, walking alone
with my mind,
without my heart
that I left there,
Buried next to the jasmine of the house
so that I could soon return,
as I cannot bear staying away for long.
And as long as I stay away from there,
the age counter decreases in return,
like an hourglass contemplating its end,
and fearing it,
knowing that with the last
grain of sand that will fall,
the heart will stop,
and will not return.
And the jasmine will cry for you for forty days,
then will bow from the cruelty of mourning
and the loneliness of loss
to die next to you.

Dr. Ali Tawil, Gaza, Palestine

Palestine, My Palestine

Palestine will be free... Every inch and olive tree

All the children we will save... from the river to the sea

We'll resist, we won't fear, everyone you and me

Israel can't kill us while... you and I watch and see

For every crime they commit... Israel will pay a fee

We are rooted in the land... our homes we won't flee

We shall not leave them alone... A united Ummah is a key

All for one, one for all... we are a single family tree

Occupation will go away... no more stings from the bee

When we get our victory, we will have kunafa and tea.

Raaya Elzamzamy, USA

Lost Child

She sits in a pile of rubble calling out
Wondering why no one is about.
She doesn't understand what is going on.
Her favourite colour is all around,
 even on her hands red is found.
Not a soul to hold her hand,
 only the footsteps and laughter of the evil men.
Tears flow, pain is numb.
The little girl spots her dead mum.
She crawls to the lifeless body, and holds it tight
"whispering mummy can I sleep here with you tonight".
As she closes her eyes a smile appears,
as she feels Allah is near.

Bibi Ashia Akhtar

Why Why Why

Why the bombing?
Why the killing?
Why could the Palestinians just stay living?
Why does there have to be all this commotion?
Why does Palestine have to feel all this emotion?

We can't just boycott we have to protest to save Palestine from all this mess
We cannot forget the past 76 years there has been so much hurt and so any tears
We keep Palestine in our prayers and find a way to show that we care.

Our loved ones are unnecessarily being bombed in Gaza, Westbank and Lebanon
Life if short but theirs became shorter from so much unjust but their spirits will not be crushed
Gaza is screaming there is nowhere left to hide now can we just stop this genocide.

All the joy was taken in the first bomb
How can the world just let this carry on?
Dropping bomb after bomb after bomb after bomb!

Aria-Rose Harper (age 9)

Palestine Palestine

If I had a magic wand I would save the people of Palestine,
I would help them get the aid they need to ease the pain inside,
I would get them food to help them heal and wipe away their tears.

The people of Gaza old and young need every bit of help,
Now with my magic wand let me scream at the top of my lungs,
Save the people in Palestine from Gaza to Westbank!
Let's save them with my magic wand and save them from these tanks.

The Palestinians shouldn't have to go through daily death and pain.
This will be felt for years to come, and the world will call your name.
I want to see you all smile again,I will not let you fall.

Palestine you will be free, I have my magic wand,
To come and let your lives be safe away from all these bombs.
Netanyahu you do not speak for me and you never will,
I will call out this genocide and all these people you have killed.

To name a few beautiful lives that have been lost
Hala, Hind, Sidra, Reem, Iman the list goes on and on
Please everyone who will survive you are so so very strong.

There may not be a magic wand but I do have my voice,
I will use it for good so the Palestinians cab have a choice,
The choice will be to live in your homeland safely day and night.

Sit tight Palestinians I am here using my voice and making it loud and clear,

I love you Palestine, I love you uncle Yo, you all deserve to live and I shall make that so.

Aria-Rose Harper (age 9)

My Gaza Dream

I dare to dream,
The Muslim in me,
Of the day when ummah will be set free,
From this hellish pain and pharaonic tyranny.

I dare to dream,
The Muslim in me,
That Palestine will indeed be set free,
From the river to the sea.

I dare to dream,
The Muslim in me,
The mutilated babies of Gaza,
Will no longer be pulled from under the rubble.

I dare to dream,
The Muslim in me,
That the martyrs are rejoicing,
In the company of Ibrahim (AS),
Eagerly waiting to welcome you and me.

I dare to dream,
The Muslim in me,
Of a strengthened ummah,
A United ummah,
The strongest ummah,
The inheritors of Jannah.

Hiba Anwer Moten

The Silence of Law

I stood in halls where voices rise,
In defense of truth beneath cold skies.
I learned the laws that bind the fight,
The codes that promise wrong and right.

But in the quiet, I began to see,
The rules are bent, they don't apply to me.
I was taught of justice, peace, and care,
But where is it when death fills the air?

In Gaza's streets, the bombs still fall,
Where is the law? Does it stand at all?
The Geneva pages, the treaties signed,
Seem lost to history, erased from mind.

We study how to wage a war with grace,
But not what happens when we lose our place.
When bombs fall harder than we ever planned,
Who speaks for the broken, for the sand?

I wear the uniform, I bear the name,
But there's a weight that cannot be tamed.
How can I stand for peace and law,
When every action makes the truth withdraw?

I think of my son, his innocent eyes,
Of how he'll grow and wonder why.
Will he ask me of Gaza, of pain untold,
Or wonder why the world's grown cold?

I dream of him running, full of joy,
Not of fear, not of broken toys.
I hold him close, I shield him tight,
But what will I tell him when he asks, "Why the fight?"

The cries of Gaza reach my soul,
A soldier bound by a distant goal.
But what of justice? What of right?
When bombs are dropped under the cover of night.

I teach him lessons of honor and care,
But how do I teach him to repair
A world where silence speaks so loud,
Where innocence is lost in a bloodied crowd?

The world watches, but does not speak,
As the cries of Gaza grow soft and weak.
I, a soldier, now see the cost—
A war for peace, but peace is lost.

May we find the courage to break this chain,
To lift the cries of those in pain.
For the law that we study, the truth we embrace,
Should serve the living, not just the race.

And as a father, I make this plea,
That my son may live in a world that's free,
Where love is the answer, not the fight—
A world where justice finds the light.

For Gaza, justice, and humanity.

Major Hidayat Muhamad,
Malaysian Army

Tents

Tents.
Burnt tents
A silhouette.
A boy.
Trapped.
IV drip attached.
A boy.
Trapped.
The mind asks the heart
The heart asks the mind.
Was this an illusion?
Surely not true.
IV drip attached.
Red.
Blaze
Moist eyes.
Sunken soul.
I thought we said lest we forget
How did we forget.
Shaban Al Dalu…your silent cries in the Al Aqsa Hospital make shift tents acting as your hospital
ward…I will not forget.
For you, for Reem, Rafhat, Maryam and thousands more, I will not forget.
Tents.
Your tent will haunt me.
Your tent will raise you.
Your tent gives you Martyrdom.
Sleep free.
For you are now free.

Repi Begum

Remorse of a witness

I'm crushed under
my soft pillow.
I can't handle
the comfort of wiping my eyes

with a napkin.

I looked up at the clock: six-thirty
Should catch the school bus, my boy

while the other says feeling thirty,
cries over how to take care of his sisters.
No more fun of sibling fights,
No more morning rush in joy.

Sleeping so deeply, my little girl

her hands falling into the emptiness—
Real as death, that emptiness.
But how? That tiny girl in Gaza with curls
must be only sleeping, as well.
Her cheeks sunken in—
once chased by mom to eat more,
her cheeks, her mom... no more.

My sweet kindergartner

running to hug me after school.
But her sweet peer is now

wrapped in a white sheet on the floor

like a candy packet, but sour.
What earth can take in so much candy?

Which mind, which conscience could?
Turns out, they could do more.

I witnessed and became a part of

a genocide.

Those who didn't

threw themselves into the fire.
My pillow and my napkin held me back—
I couldn't.
I couldn't fight back.

Ayse Meryem, Istanbul, Turkiye

O Dear World

O Dear World,
Since that 7th noon,
I am limping[1] around in complete distress by foot & heart.
Blood pours on me while I am deep asleep
The insides of me scream to a degree my soul shrieks
No, I don't want to laugh at the joke you cracked,
while my people wrecked under the rubble of the houses they once slept.
An ocean flows from my eyes, dawn to dusk
I turn myself to comprehend faces here and there
Is there humanity left anywhere?
And every time I get a glimpse of them,
I feel restless, helpless- a surging apocalypse within me.
An ache that sores with each passing day,
as I see black smoke of people thinning in the air,
Heartaches filling starvation
"Death has arrived early", they say
O World, is there a way to customize amnesia?
My hope's at the brink, rushed to refill
saw my kith n kin killed.
What pollution, What feminism, What etiquettes, What humanity, you talk of, all year round?
The cry of the innocents beat me to the ground
Tell me, how loud should I scream, for you to see?
Tell me, how much should I limp, for you to hear?

---

1 Al-Nu'man ibn Bashir reported: The Messenger of Allah, peace and blessings be upon him, said, "The parable of the Ummah in their affection, mercy, and compassion for each other is that of a body. When any limb aches, the whole body reacts with sleeplessness and fever." Source: Ṣaḥīḥ al-Bukhārī 6011, Ṣaḥīḥ Muslim 2586

~ In the light of this hadith, I am limping because Prophet Muhammad ﷺ said that Ummah is one body, when one part experiences pain, so does the other. I am limping because my heart (ġaza) is bleeding.

Tell me, how should I write for you to know?
& if you can't tell,
please show humanity hasn't bid farewell!

Shifa Mohammad Munshi

Palestine: Our Strawberry Farm

People talk of roots,
People talk of struggle,
People hide their ignorance.
People help fund inhumanity.

Society is unfair to certain people,
Society reproduces the cycle,
Society has to learn to redistribute or in this case, re-allocate back to its rightful owner.
Palestine is Palestine and my family's roots.

No more migration,
Immigration,
Or intimidation,
It is time for some litigation.

People talk of my roots,
Let's all put on our walking boots.
And go back to our fruits.

Dr Shrehan Lynch, London, UK

Boundaries of Longing

1. (To the occupation soldier)
If I were a bird,
Your borders could not stop me.
1. (To whom it may concern)
If I were a bird
With two wings
I
Would not wake up from
my dreams.
Yet,
I would sail in the pure sky,
Then fly,
While there are no missiles,
No smoke shapes
No labored breaths, or moans,
or women's screams,
That buzz in our ears
every day.
"
I
Would fly
To another sky,
That returns my missed concepts,
Or maybe, missed senses,
I'm searching, sir,
In my slumber, in my waking,
I'm searching for it, sir.
In my whisper, in my touch
I'm my past, in my present.
And equally in my future.

No one has to disclose me,
Here, sir;
No one heeds me,
the emotions I had,
or, on my beloved land!
No one here is
Giving me the compass of the unknown.
Sir, give me the gaunt maze map in its way.
"
Give me a signal to draw by my hand.
It's rustle, as a map.
Putting my land, my town,
and my beloved country space,
in the spot, authentic place!
Give me a signal,
to rebuild its crushed edifices,
As it should be,
to make arrival so feasible.
"
Sir, give me a profound breath.
that enables me
to wake from my deep coma.
Give me an hour,
In my lovely home, and my room
To hold my extensive scatteredness on
The side extreme,
then I taste the sweetness spent hours.
And smell the scent of flowers, that,
Alas!
I have left, yet still have their
nostalgia thorns.
"

Give me what I have lost,
In the bloodiest way, so then
I promise
To give you PEACE,
Because, sir,
What I have lost,
I will, in ample way,
Freely give to you.

Fatena Abu Mostafa, Gaza, Palestine

Unreachable North, Unbreakable Bonds

Between me and the north of this city
Overflowing asking,
Overflowing answering,
full of words
with huge emotions.
Between me and the north of this city,
long streets, yet
short streets,
war indeed diverges them.
Between me and the north of this city,
a lot of sea faces,
a lot of sky faces.
Between me and the north of this city,
unlimited borders, built by force,
to kill the stories of friends,
to pick up the discarded smiles,
and throw them a distance.
Between me and the north of this city,
unlimited friends gathering,
full of watery eyes,
eyes of beloveds,
saved in clouds;
waiting at the terminal of the Holocaust,
to cast out the clouds,
to let fall these tears.
Between me and the north of this city.
an embrace that never fades.
Tears gather like rain clouds above,
falling softly along my cheeks,
as the memory of parting
stirs anew in my heart.

Between me and the north of this city,
unforgettable hours at Scopes,
witnesses positions,
for infinite learning gatherings,
for infinite dreaming plans,
for infinite clapping hands,
where my achievements were performed.
Between me and the north of this city,
My home, my room
My neighbors and their tears
My fruits on the trees
in the yard of my home
all of them waiting for me.
Between me and the north of this city,
My latest hope, My last dream,
that broke on my bed.
Recounting my day to mom in the kitchen,
gathering to play games with my neighbors' kids
in the garden.
my books of tales,
books of fancy,
books of Heracles.
My present,
My past,
My future
All of them between me and the north of this city
All of them stuck in my brain.
The sights, the signs
hopeful sensations,
of approaching recurrence.

Fatena Abu Mostafa, Gaza, Palestine

Never ask me again

Never ask me
How's my life
If you do not have a chance
to prevent my pain
let me explain
and then you can obtain
the way you can help my brain
to keep its consciousness.
My tears have dried up
Give me a tear, to relieve the pain of dryness in my heart.
Give me a drop,
to extinguish the fire burning what's left of me.
Teach me how to throw my grief.
Look at my heart;
help me to extract all the scars.
Teach me how to fly,
to be able to fly
as birds fly.
Give me new feet that
lead me to the peace that I miss.
Take me far away,
to my friends in a peaceful place.
Take me to paradise,
to see them another time.
To have my old smile again,
to breathe again
to taste the feeling of comfort,
that I've never tasted.
Take me to my beloved persons above,

and I promise
to save you a seat.
If you can't
Go away from me,
and never ask me again.

Fatena Abu Mostafa, Gaza, Palestine

It is not easy lifting the souls of Gaza

It's not easy for us,
To witness the unraveling of humanity,
To see a genocide etched into the earth,
To hear the whispers of the silenced,
Their names swept away like dust.
Not easy,
To lift the souls of Gaza on our shoulders,
To march with hearts heavy as gravestones,
Carrying their cries in our throats,
Their dreams in our steps.
Signs, flags, banners and kites raised high,
Letters sharp as broken glass:
Freedom, Justice, Life.
But what do these words mean,
When the world turns its back?
Props of dead bodies sway in the wind,
Tiny hands painted on cardboard,
Small feet marching along
With eyes wide with questions
That elders never found their answers.
Buggies roll past,
Not with sleeping children,
But with ghosts of their smiles and laughter,
The weight of innocence lost.
It's not easy,
making props of dead children
Heavier than their souls
To face the firestorm of indifference,
To meet the gaze of power unmoved,

To lead a small march
To hold the grief that spills from every corner
Of a land strangled by despair.
But still we march,
From Swindon to Gaza
We march for Justice we chant
Bearing witness,
Bearing the unbearable,
Because their voices must not fade,
Because we carry more than pain—
We carry hope
We carry the souls of Gaza on our shoulders

Fadoua Govaerts

The Guilt of Motherhood

I look at my children, their faces so pure,
Their laughter a comfort, but something feels unsure.
I am their mother, their guide, their shield,
Yet all I feel is the weight that this world won't yield.

I buy their socks with a guilt in my chest,
Knowing there are children who have no rest.
I give them gifts, not too much, not too few,
But in my heart, I know what's been taken from you.

Their birthdays should sparkle, their joy should be free,
But inside I wonder, "What kind of world will they see?"
How can I make them feel special, when I know the cost,
When others are suffering, everything feels lost?

Each celebration feels hollow, each cheer bittersweet,
For I know that somewhere, children can't feel their feet.
I tell them "You're precious," but my soul feels the strain,
For in Gaza, the children can't even remain.

Nothing feels right, not a single thing,
How do you celebrate when the world's not offering?
I carry my children, yet they feel the weight,
Of a mother's guilt and a world of hate.

They ask me questions, their eyes full of trust,
And I try to shield them from all that's unjust.
But how do I teach them the world isn't fair,

When I'm still struggling with the reality that I can't bear?
I protest, I shout, I march with my kin,
But none of it feels enough, not a thing.
The money I raise, the voices I lend,
All seem so small when there's no end.

And then I look at my children, their faces so bright,
And feel the ache in my chest, the endless fight.
They see my tears, they feel my dismay,
And I think of all the mothers in Gaza each day.

The guilt of motherhood weighs me down,
Mothers experiencing daily grief, in tears they drown,
Continuing as usual does not feel right,
Every school run, club or meal becomes a burden a fight.

In every celebration, in every gift I give,
I feel I'm failing them, how can I live?
Knowing that nothing feels enough to repay,
The mothers in Gaza who've lost all they hold dear every day.

And still, I carry on, my love or fight never stops,
But the guilt of motherhood fills every thought.
The failure of humanity and world silence is hard
Gaza must be rebuild with children's laughter on every yard

Dr Fadoua Govaerts

The Keffiyeh in the Crowd

A thousand faces fill the room, a sea of shifting tides,
Lost amidst the thrumming hum, where empty echoes hide.
"Leave your baggage at the door," their cheerful voices say,
But all I see are haunted scenes that will not fade away.

Children huddle beneath torn tents, their books worn thin with dust,
Learning truths the world denies, their dreams held firm with trust.
"Education is a right," the speakers boldly claim,
Yet I see no education but children etched in pain

I search the crowd for kindred souls, for hearts that bear the weight,
For those who know the ache of loss, the scars that won't abate.
Until at last, amidst the throng, a symbol catches light—
A keffiyeh, bold and woven strong, a beacon in the night.

You are one of me, I think, your gaze reflects my own,
You carry stories in your soul that cannot be disowned.
In this place of dissonance, you offer me reprieve,
A silent pact, a kindred bond, a reason to believe.

But then I see another there, a keffiyeh draped with pride,
A stranger yet familiar, carrying the fight inside.
And one by one, they start to show, each thread a woven plea,
We're searching for each other now, for solidarity.
We meet with trembling hands that reach, our voices cracking raw,

A hug, a cry, a moment shared—we recognise the law:
The strategy to silence hope, to cleanse and brutalise,
The genocide that strips their homes and crushes hopes for education's rise.

The keffiyeh speaks of dignity, of virtue unbowed by fear,
A thread of hope in resistance sewn, steadfast and sincere.
It defies the tides of erasure, the silencing of screams,
It stands for those whose stolen homes are carried in their dreams.

We gather in this crowded space, a quiet, solemn chain,
Each keffiyeh a banner raised against a world of pain.
Together we resist the lies, the cleansing, the despair,
We stand for every voice suppressed, no matter when or where.

Through hugs and tears, we form a bond, a family born of fight,
The keffiyeh our collective flame, a symbol burning bright.
As long as one is left to wear its steadfast folds with pride,
The struggle for justice lives, unbroken, undenied.

Dr Fadoua Govaerts

As the sun comes up ?

As the sun comes up and then the moon
They pray that the dust will settle soon
They have no food, not even water
They try and hide from the ongoing slaughter
They have to watch their loved ones die
Right in front of their very eyes
The bombs are loud and very close
Blood on the street once again flows
The innocent hunt amongst the rubble
They never asked for any of this trouble
All they can do is let the world see
And pray that soon they will be forever free

Francesca Vowles, Trowbridge UK)

And Samson Wept – Eyeless in Gaza

Eyeless in Gaza was Samson then.
Now eyeless in Gaza many, many more again.

Eyeless, and homeless, limbless and lifeless, in Gaza today.
No matter the suffering the innocent must pay.

Electronic eyes watch but cannot tell.
Others have eyes but cannot see the hell.

Camera eyes tell but do not speak
Unable to act on the cries of the weak.

Blind to suffering, day after day
With guilty eyes, the world looks away.

Homes brought down
Bodies under ground
Parents mourn,
children just born.

Helpless, homeless, eyeless in Gaza once more.
How strange, how blind such rules of war.

An eye for an eye. One tooth for one tooth.
Yet many thousand deaths are not enough.

There: eyeless in Gaza,
Where Samson once wept.

Bryn Jones, Bath, UK

I am Gaza.

I am Gaza
As destroyed as can ever be.
I am Gaza you'll never forget about me.
I am Gaza Once I was free
Remember when you named gauze after me?

I am Gaza now all rubble.
once full of hope laughter and joy
I am Gaza with Nothing left to destroy

I am Gaza with all its dust corpses and rubble
The trauma, the cries the blood the trouble
I know what you see on your screens is beyond imagination
Yet Not enough to stop it by the United Nations

I am Gaza the dove representing peace.
what I witnessed is horrifying at its very least
feeling the power of the bombs in the sky and the trees
Heading north south west and east

I am Gaza I am Palestine. I will never die.
The massacred children in heaven they fly
The mothers and fathers crying in pain
Their blood will not ever be in vain

I am Gaza I am Palestine. Occupied for 75 years
Oppressed, deprived, rivers filling my tears
I won't give up my human rights
I am Gaza I will use my tears and rocks to fight.

I am Gaza. Our voices and cries have been heard.
Now you must be my messenger bird.
I am Gaza. I demand you to act against this genocide
Before any peace, justice will be on our side

Asiya Ali (13) UK

I wonder

When you look into their dead, cold, blank faces,
What is it you feel I wonder as you leave with plenty a trace?

Do you feel sorrow? Guilt? Or even shame?
For you know that you are cursed and will not be the same

I wonder and think a lot about your mind
But of course the supporters are worse for pretending to be blind.

You laugh at the dead child in its bed.
You dance and mock. you know your hands are forever stained with red.

I cry for them to be freed
But it is sectioning and sanctions you need.

You must be crazed if you think this is right
Are you serious? Bombing the innocent at night?

You say you are being oppressed as if anyone will believe that!
And some pretend to be victims and under threat. But those people are no better than a scruffy rat.

As I write this poem in grave disgust imagining all the crimes you cover up
You say you give them water. When the water is not enough to fill a cup.

You say you give them food.
Weren't you taught lying is quite rude?

You should be ashamed. You shouldn't be able to sleep.
When the truth is. The community you have sowed, is about to be reaped.

Palestinians for years endured the price and pain
for resisting and steadfast in their land you claim

I would say you deserve torture and suffering for what you did to who you couldn't tame.
But I will leave justice to be served by them who will look at you with disgust and shame.

I wonder, would you keep your head high or low?
When people shout at you in turn. Row by row.

For those settlements of yours do not even belong to you!
The farmer didn't know he was to be murdered but of course. You knew.

You kill without emotion, without shame.
Do you even remember their names?

The names of the people you randomly chose to kill. The children you tortured
Of course not. For there are too many to count.
And still your hands become reddened.

I wait for the politicians to finally wake up from this daze
For they say ok to you even when they only see through a haze.

Do I need to elaborate? Do I need to explain?
For the only thing you have been generous with is pain.

This is the end of this mere tiny poem. But do not stop as the sentence finishes.
But keep fighting for all those poor *dead* childrens' wishes.

Asiya Ali (13) UK

In our eyes

Look straight in our eyes!
Look at the families who died!
See through our pain!
What was there to gain?
When we die another takes place to stand their ground,
So there is no point of trying to murder our hope all round!
Look straight in our eyes,
We all know their tricks and lies
See through our tears and pain !
This was never some silly game!
When one of us dies we still live,
What we all know is that they will never win!
The moment they started this with great cost,
They should've known that they had already lost.
And when we say the start we don't mean the 7th,
Because how many were murdered before and flew off to heaven?
Look straight in our eyes!
We can see through their fake cries.
See our real cries and blood,
Our tears become a flood
When we are buried our seed is planted,
Our seed grows into a tree that is enchanted.
Look at how we've grown!
That is nothing they would've known
If we collected every drop of blood we shed,
The entire world would be covered in a deep dark red.
Even if all of us were to die,
Our voices will be heard from the sky!
all of the children witnessing their family die,

The children are sad as they watch them fly.
After all our evidence and rage,
The people still ignore our cries for days!
Take this as a meaningful sign!
For if your leader is wrong, step out of line!
Be our voices as we are your eyes and ears,
Explain our pain to all of your fellow peers.
We plead for them the friends to look in our eyes
To our friends on the other side of river Nile who hear our cries
These are not words of one person in a couple of a mile,
These are the voices of our people on the other side of river Nile.
My name is Hind Rajab I am but six years old
I am alive through my story people have told
My name is Hind Rajab. I may just be a mere six year old
But I apparently know better than what those politicians have on hold

Asiya Ali (13) UK

Cry Gaza

Here I sit
On my sofa
Sipping frothy coffee;
Blind to the noise
The Cry, despair;
Of another human,
A million human !Humanity itself.

Shame on you !
May your head hang
So low
It touches
Your heart;
And your
heart
Cries::
As it knows.
Gaza !
Gaza !
Gaza !

Then you have
Earned to live
Truly as a human being;
Not just
Flesh, bones & blood.
Cry out
In pain
And with love.

Loud and clear
Let your heart
Burst out !
Till all cries meet
Rise, moves
Changes the world.
Gaza !
Gaza !
Gaza !

Beas Bhattacharya, Bath, UK

One blood, one Freedom

I cut my hand
In the kitchen knife.
Blood drips through my fingers.
Blood speaks
More than words....

I sense the blood stained Streets of Gaza.
The last resort hide - outs ,
Abandoned,strewn apart
Families
Abu, Ammi, Tifl
Lost, taken or
Unknown.

Fight for freedom !
Soil, earth ,country
Home.
Now is
A fight to breath, to survive !
One morsel of food
One caring hand
One voice
One glance ....

Trickle of blood
Flows, relentless
Like a river
As tears dries up,
Mouths parched,

Yet
An ocean is forming
Vast.
Invincible.
Listen and
You can hear
It's roar !.

Beas Bhattacharya, Bath, UK

A Morning like No Other,

Off to Yorkshire, to Wild Wood Cottage,
When Alexa's voice cuts through the calm:

**"It began with a barrage of at least 2,200 rockets in just 20 minutes,
providing cover for at least 1,500 militants
who infiltrated Israel at dozens of points."**

Oh, shit. This is massive.
All day, behind the wheel, my mind is racing.
We need to do something.
The media screams—**beheaded babies,**
but I can't trust it, they lie, they lie,
IsraeHell it›s all a lie.

We March, We Protest, We cry.

We stand in the cold, the wet, the wind, the sun,
under winter skies, under cherry blossoms,
under summer sun, and autumn leaves.
Days, Weeks, Months, a Year,
still they lie, and lie, and lie.

We Stand. We March. We Cry.

My world bleeds red, black, green, and white
colours that haunt my waking hours.
Tunnels, Hospitals, Schools,
the lie is repeated, over and over again.
They lie. They lie. They lie.

War crimes. War crimes. War Crimes.

My only weapon my voice, my camera, my eyes,
to witness the truth, to document the response.
Genocide Joe and Zionist Starmer,
feeding the war machine,
fattening the pockets of arms companies while families starve.

Red lines in Cities, Children's clothes on beaches,
shopping centres, body bags of babies,in borrowed pushchairs,
struggling to break through the noise.
Still, They lie, They lie, They lie.

Week in, Week out,

We March, We Stand, We Cry.

Johnny T Fox , Swindon, UK

THE GREAT RETURN

Oh beloved, soil of my land!
When I return to you, I return not alone,
But with the remains of weaponry
That reek with fear
Of the Invaders who used it against me.

He feels terror,
when he sees me walk this ground everyday-
With his sniper,
And his shield,
And his bombs and his rockets and his missiles
Waiting for the right time - the command in his earpiece.

I have nothing,
But the honour to fight back with you.

I pick up the rocks you left behind for me
And I throw it at them on your behalf.

I can see the anger in their eyes turn into dread,
Though they pretend it's rage-
Because they realize,
They cannot take a land that does not want to be taken.

So when I come to you, I come with pride,
Because to be a part of you is to fight back-
For the next rock that is thrown,
could be taken from my grave.

Long Live Resistance!

Ira Khalid

335 Bullets 335

(phone call between 6yr old Hind Rajab stuck in car and Aid worker)

Doctors' waiting lists long in UK
Hospitals bombed and raided in Gaza
Ambulances used as beds in UK
Ambulances shot at, blown up, non-existent in Gaza

Where are you hiding now?
In the car ... 335

UK Health Service jobs galore
Gaza Blood and gore; Medics, sniper crosshairs
Supermarket Asda free soup for UK pensioners
Humanitarian Aid, cut and blocked for Palestinians

I won't hang up OK?
The tank, the tank is next to me ... 335

Free data sim cards for UK people in poverty
Remote explosion mobiles for Hezbollah
UK "Freedom for Palestine" calls, fall on deaf ears
Apartheid Genocide Palestinian prisoners, far from free

OK don't be scared
Please stay with me ... 335

Widespread internet access in UK
Internet cut and blocked in Gaza West Bank
Meals on Tik Tok in UK; on Tik Tok in Gaza
Bodies mutilated, bodies mummified; Press Corps cross-haired

I will not leave you alone
Please come take me, please ... 335

On worldwide mobile phones and news reports
minute by minute, Palestinian Apocalypse continues
UK, Middle East and Worldwide Politicians
lip-service any caring, with bloodstained daggers still drawn

It's almost night I'm scared
Sweetie I swear, if I could, I would, come and get you ... 335

Tony Hillier, Swindon, UK

on catastrophe

catastrophe; there is no time
but hunger left.
what has happened, has happened
will happen again.
have leaves, have grass
and the flour spilled
from your uncle's arms
the day he was murdered in line.
where do they come from - the creatures of decay?
no one eats here but them,
feeding on lifeless limbs,
gnawing at ash-crusted bone;
rags to dust
what was once a human,
but you are not humans here -
they are not humans there.
they stare at the stars beyond the warplanes.
the sky never belonged to anyone
and neither did the Earth;
we non-humans belong to catastrophe.
nothing lives, no-one lives
for the place they were birthed to lay perished,
for the water itself to leech them
of sustenance, of promise.
how the babies scream for milk
atop their mother's dried breast
who pray now only to die
together with their children.
to Ihab, the six-year-old boy who slept beneath a truck,

his plum-sized heart knowing catastrophe had been robbing
him of innocence since the womb
and had now taken his family too -
he slept to die, he died as he slept
in unbearable cold on his concrete bed.
to live is to die, to die is a number
we watch rise, multiply, still hunger
knows no bounds
as the threshold for humanitarianism
remains in the clouds
for their own judgement, their own approval.
we watch it unfold,
remain proudly principled
as they find shrivelled stomachs
in bomb-ridden hospitals.
on catastrophe pin
collective sympathy, do nothing,
eat away at time
find it wasting, racing
away into the hands of the oppressor
readying their blood-soaked flag
to plant on the ransacked land
rancid with hunger of their own
to match that of the girl trapped in the car
on the line for us all to hear
as she called out to reach her
Hind
was she not starving too?
was she not starving too?
or was it a tragedy?
was Gaza a shelter
to be shaken, not lamented?

was Gaza the price we were happy to pay

for ignominy, bargaining parity

for our catastrophic, colonising need for a peace

that grows on the muddle of bodies and tombstones, tombstones and bodies;

were they not starving too?

were they not starving too?

Memoona Ahmed, Oxford, UK

Winter Hill

As I walk out in winter's calm
High on a brumal hill
Still naked trees jut
While the world whirls
Its madness

Through their Stygian branches
Gun metal sky
Shot with bloody smears
Of a dying sun
Strafes my eyes

On the far horizon
A bead is drawn
On these frosted fields
And as I tread the rime
My peace is shattered
By what I know to be
Far from here
In Palestine

D.R.Sweeney Wiltshire, UK.

Weep for the Little Children

In a distant land
Through a narrow strip
Between wall and sea
A monster rampages
Ravaging innocent
Starving masses
Leaving carnage in its wake
Streets awash with blood and tears
While the world watches

The land is rent
The sound of the ocean
Drowned by drones
Through endless nights of terror
Dreams are robbed
Homes murdered
Pounded to rubble
Crumpled cities
Entomb untold numbers
Dead and alive

The moon that lights
The night time raids
Shining here benign
Draws the ocean there
To lap the shore
Yet all the water
In that vast sea
Is insufficient

To wash the blood from the hands
Who feed the greedy
Power crazed monster
Killer of innocents

Weep for the little children
Dead by morning
See their tiny bodies
Wrapped in bloody shrouds
Cradled in the arms of broken hearts
Lain in the street with no-one to name them
Their mothers could not save them
For they were murdered too
Buried in their homes

D.R.Sweeney Wiltshire, UK.

Olive Tree

The tree could have lived
To one thousand years old
A symbol of peace and strength to behold
Its roots in the ground, winter and summer
Standing strong and firm; year after year, another, another
But this tree is not invincible, though hard to defeat
75 years of occupation, its strength bound to deplete
Those strong roots have made the land its home like mine and yours
Only so much displacement, occupation and murder they can endure
The fruit that bloomed and the oil that was made to nourish
In a state of genocide and horror, there's no room to flourish
A species, a people that are known to be so resilient and strong
One that lives and grows on the land that they belong
But why should it matter where your roots meet the ground?
In which country or continent that you have been found?
Long live Palestine and the great olive tree
Until Palestine has peace, no one truly can be free

Emily Masi-Cacchio

Poor Palestine

How can you laugh at dead babies?
Dead children?
How?
It makes me cry it makes me sad and what is watching tv and crying going to do to stop the genocide?
To stop the bombing?
What will it do?
Nothing!
When I say I don't like this food I remember Gaza has no food no water nothing.
When my mum gets mad at me and I get upset at her I remember babies have no mama left.
No baba left.
The only piece of mama and baba is the rubble it makes me cry.
I can't believe Israel looks for children looking for food and kill them.
And then laugh how dare they.
I cry when they die and so do they

Lola Ali (age 7)

Baby Boy

A baby boy's head is filled with dreams
and the possibilities of first words...
But look closer and you see
the baby's head is empty,
beside it on the bed-
its brain and dreams splayed across
The soft nurturing blanket,
the soft nurturing mother.

Orlaith O'Neill, Wiltshire

Daddy's girl

Dad carries his little girl in his arms like you do
when they fall asleep before bedtime.
Gently climbing up the steps
made of walls and roofs and families.
Her older brother holds her hand,
walking behind, and carries it back to Mom
So she will have more of her daughter's
flesh to weep over.

Orlaith O'Neill (Wiltshire)

How?

How do you hold your dignity as protectively
As an infant or a skinny kitten?
How do you hold your pain so courageously
As we pray for the sea of it to part?
How do you hold your love as fiercely
As the deeds to your nobility?
How do you clutch your smiles so closely
As an old precious key about your heart?
How do you speak so eloquently
As our throats are bursting with rage?
How do you hold hope aloft so often
As a beacon from your darkness?
How are you teaching us to be human,
Again?

Orlaith O'Neill (Wiltshire)

Raging Love

I am not consumed by the fire of rage
But hold it in my hands
And tenderly place love into palms
to soothe the heat
I am not consumed by the fire of rage
But hold it in my hands, in love
Feeling the burn of fury
as it blisters
accepting its place in me
An emotion within my influence
It is a part of love
held for the suffering

I breathe on the red flame,
offering the white light of love
Rage bends, but never flickers
-It has a right to be here

I breathe love onto it,
and it softens, transforms,
red to white, but never flickers
-Adapting but resolute

Another breath,
momentum to begin the journey over there
Sends this raging white flame of love
Of healing
Of peace

And the flame rises, mighty and tall,
An unstoppable inferno of raging love
The winds know what love speaks of
And they carry the flame
Over there, to wrap them in love.

Orlaith O'Neill (Wiltshire)

The recycling of Palestinians

We'll recycle this one into dust
And that one into fumes
This one into soil
And that one we'll exhume to recycle
 into food for the poor scavenging dogs
This one will be the contents of a plastic bag
That one a tiny coffin
This one wouldn't fill a sandwich bag
No, they don't get buried whole often...

This one will become infill for the hole we made
With bombs America and Germany donated
"But we need more....
The hole is big
and there are too many of them!"

There are sufficient Palestinians, still
to be recycled into bomb hole infill.
And O! How green we'll be and how wonderful we
with our carbon bootprint
on their faces.

Orlaith O'Neill (Wiltshire)

Shaban al-Dalou

We watched him burn, flames crawling from his neck to his skull
He watched himself burn, smelled himself burn, heard himself burn
The sizzle of Palestinian flesh no longer a sin,
apparently.
(- or is that fucking blood libel?)

It felt rude, not knowing his name
While watching his people try and fail
To extinguish the fire that ate through his bones.
We found out after
His name was Shaban.

Shaban, I'm sorry for the intimacy forced upon you
As the world watched your agony, saw you consumed
I'm sorry that you died screaming before my eyes
Your bones cracking, your friends wailing, your people
Genocided - butchered, slaughtered

O your cries,
and mine, and billions more besides.
And us without a name to offer a prayer for.

Shaban, brother, noble human, burned alive by "The West"
May your name always ignite the flame of truth, of humanity, of change.
Your name that tells of Arab tribes dispersing to search for water and food.
Oh how your name is true!

Always remember Shaban al-Dalou.

Orlaith O'Neill (Wiltshire)

The Terrorist of Bil'in

There once was a woman who once had a home
Surrounded by olive trees and flowers she'd grown
Now the garden was stolen - her trees torn apart
But she knew that their strength carried on in her heart
So she turned new ground and planted new seeds
With love for the flowers that would surely appear

Her plant pots were gone, with the house and the trees
So she collected grenades that lay on the street
She cleaned and filled them with hope, soil and seeds
Their purpose transformed from war into peace
In this act of resistance, sniper focus clear
She terrorised pain and made a hostage of fear

A resistance to war a resistance to doom
A manifesto for hope with each flower that blooms
Adding fire to fire increases the flame
So the blaze burns hotter and so does the blame
She chose to nourish her own peace instead
And spread it, with love, from those former grenades.

Orlaith O'Neill (Wiltshire)

This our story

This is our story, to tell in our own way.
We alone decide who's seen and who should have their say.
We have the power for a reason, our voice respected and refined.
Our privilege to choose what's known and what we need to hide.

We script this pantomime, in our righteous pen and ink,
To be taken as it's seen, without the need to think.
Leave alone your questions, you have no part to play.
Do not find another angle or spell it another way.

No need to dupe the many; we stir the foolish, court the strong.
We'll set the bar to decide what is right and wrong.
We have the method to convince, the wealth to purchase love,
The tools to smear dissenters and risk their livelihoods.

In our cloak of virtue, we'll harangue at centre stage,
And colonise your language, to re-define each phrase.
We'll demonise your every word, impound them one by one,
Till your message is unspeakable, voiceless and alone.

Don't think of speaking up, or we'll make you break the law,
We can change the laws to do this, that's what our influence is for.
And we'll unleash armies of hungry baited beasts,
Who've lost themselves and must fill the hole with something to defeat.

We'll celebrate half-truths and lies with big bright flashing lights,
And bury inconvenient facts completely out of sight.
The strong and powerful we'll portray as pained,
Pitch those oppressed as to be feared and blamed.

We will choose who matters, in our reverential reign,
As favoured blood is thickened by their fathers' pains,
Yet others blood is watered thin,
That can be turned on or off at the right man's whim.

One life is worth a hundred others for those who play and dress as we do,
Why resist the status quo when it's not hurting you?
Don't gaze at your sleeping child and pity those you could not save,
You're comfortable so carry on, enjoy your coffee and your cake.

Ignore the blood we smear on your hands,
We'll help distract you and dampen the sounds,
With excuses we'll mask their humanness and pain.
Look away, keep busy, save yourself the worry and the shame.

You see, your conscience is inconsequential.
Stay silently complicit, not penitential.
Tell yourself it's justified.
Tell yourself your hands are tied.

This is our story, and we get to tell it how we like.

Mindy V

The Sun – For Empathy

A plane glides over the world
Plated bottom shining
In cool
Burnished fire; set alight
In winking, silvered eye

Imagine – being so vast
So powerful and ancient
As to cast your fingers across
So many lives

And yet to scream
And scream and scream;
To tear your heart out sobbing
And leave it beating for the world to see:
A slamming, thunderous pain

To burn on
And on
And on
Throwing yourself against the glass walls of their world
Spilling your blood over
Their horizons

Only for it to kiss their faces
Mocking, as they smile up at
Your tear-shine. Laughing as they
Warm themselves in your anguish
And gilt their skin in the
Burnt shadow of your grief.

Sol Shalaby Bath, UK

Oranges

These oranges are not gilt globes - not polished, sparking jewels
Left to shine and waste and rot, dead and inert
In a lifeless, bald, sunlessness cleft and carved from home.
Here they live malformed, misshaped, mishewen
Skin rough and scared.
Uneven, unwaxed - bared, and brazen

They *thrive*, great rocky hemispheres of citrus
Bitter seeds, born to be spat into rough palms
That replant into sultry, spread, sun-warmed earth
Brewing crescents of ochre under close clipped nails

Nails scrapped under skin, nails scrapped into and within
Head lowered in prayer, into the awn of Earth, the awn of giving
Pressing mouth, kissing to the ground, thanking to the down
Before raising up to sweet pulp, sweet soft peeled pips
And springing sapped sweetness, gladly into sweat salted mouths.

Sol Shalaby Bath, UK

Gaza

imagine giving birth to a baby on the Gaza strip,

even if there where a way to track the number of births, we barley keep track of the number of deaths,

the birth place may as well say 'no mans land',

because the war is taking what rightfully belongs to falestine and hiding it with ash,

you would hope that the mother carries her baby successfully to her third trimester,

but I don't think she would feel so lucky, nevertheless childbirth is a blessing right?

WRONG! Nothing about mixing the cry's of childbirth with the screams of war is right,

Nobody has enough food to satisfy themselves let alone nurture a baby in their womb,

a mother can not honour her cravings as there are other mouths to feed,

the milk she will feed her baby will be laced with acid and famine,

childbirth is supposed to be a miracle of life but not when it is happening on the cusps of a genocide,

the baby is born kicking and screaming,

not yet knowing how to speak but already having fear present in its vocabulary,

it may be unaware why it is afraid but we all know who is too blame,

this generational trauma has started so early,

as when his eyes will clear the first thing he may see is a bomb zipping from the sky,

the question is, is the trauma of a child worth it to some?

The answer we already know is yes, the red staining the earth satisfies many as it simultaneously lines the pockets of the greedy and the hungry, that feed on the cry's of that needy baby.

The baby who's first word will be to question where his mother is
as the ringing of the bombs and sirens wails in its ears,
it brings me too tears and so for a final time i will scream,
from the land to the sea, set my people free!

Moran Hajyahya, 20

I am from Gaza.

I am from Gaza, where the earth breathes blood,
In the silence of night, the bullets sing the song of peace,
The sun rises over graves with no name,
Under them, stories burn, and dreams cease.

I am from Gaza, where planes wave and soar,
And I sleep on shards of shattered glass,
Beneath our feet, the earth swallows life,
And sorrow paves a path we must pass.

I am from Gaza, where people sway on the brink of fear,
Children lost in queues of endless hunger,
Their dreams abandoned in the streets to disappear,
And with every blast, a new dawn grows stronger.

As for me, I see only ash in the sky,
I chase after hope, despite every fall,
I hear only cries of despair, but still, I rise,
For I shall never yield, nor bow to it all.

Does their death mean we must flee?
Or does death mark the start of our tale?
Did they see weakness reflected in our eyes?
Or are we truly unbroken, in strength we prevail?
Oh, my soul, do you dream of heights above?
Or do you fear the waking from the flames of love?

But in these wounds, a heart still beats,
And in this plane, I hear your voice repeat:
"Our future is free, we shall never be bound."
Yes, we know no defeat, no sorrow will drown.

We stand, carving the future in stone,
Defying the ruin,
Challenging the beasts that cannot break our bone.
Blood cannot shatter wings,
And drowning cannot silence the songs we have sung.

Will the bodies ever fall silent, I say?
Or will words forever flow, come what may?
There will be no final death, no final loss to face,
For as time tightens, our cries will race.

I am from Gaza, and I shall remain,
Alive in memory,
A symbol of resistance,
Even when all is lost in vain.

Ibrahim Massri, Gaza, Palestine

Please Free Palestine

Peace in between Gaza and Israel
All blessings for Gaza in Palestine
Learn from your horrible mistakes Israel and free Gaza
Every dua for Palestine
Stay in Allah's protection and Insha Allah you will survive Gaza
Time to help innocent Palestinians
Israel stop bombing children and babies
No more committing murder Israel
Every Muslim donate for Gaza in Palestine

Zoraiz Fahad Syed, Swindon, UK , aged 8

Centre

At the centre of our world lies Gaza
A tiny place that changed the world
Impoverished, Besieged, Bombed and Blasted.
Sandy is the soil, and it's filled with seeds.

A home of faith, roots, courage, community
A home of humanity
A home of steadfastness.
A home of defiance.
A home, in the centre of our hearts.

Paul Menard

From the Hearts of Palestine

This is Palestine it is my home
A land where I was free to roam.
Now under occupation, I'm no longer free
But it's my land, it belongs to me.
You have no right to take my home
To push me out to call it your own.
Evil soldiers with hearts so cold
Murdering the innocent, young and old.
Bombs landing upon us day and night
Soldiers blasting us from left to right.
Mothers, fathers and children openly weep
For the loss of their loved ones, it hurts so deep.
Poor innocent children who should run free
Are left alone with no family.
No babies, no children such innocent lives
No families remain, no husbands, no wives.
The ones that are left just sit in despair
A pain so hard for them to bare.
Our happy homes are now broken and torn
Babies are killed before they are born.
The happiness that once filled our streets
Has been crushed to the ground by the soldier's feet.
But deep in our hearts we shall not fear
We know the day will soon draw near.
When God will ease our suffering and pain
And Palestine will be free once again.

Michelle Amani Darhali

A Child of Palestine

My daddy was taken by soldiers, I don't know why
I held mummy tightly as I watched her cry.
She rubbed her belly, there's a baby inside
Please don't let my baby be born tonight.
Then the bombs come falling from the sky
I heard mummy shouting, "Why? Oh why?"
I tried to reach her, but it happened so quick
There was lots of fire and smoke so thick.
Then someone came to help me and mummy
They took her away as she held her tummy.
And when I asked, are mummy and baby alright
They said they were going up to heaven tonight.
Now I'm just sitting here all alone
I have no mummy, no daddy, no home.
I'm now an orphan, a refugee
Afraid of what my future will be.
Too young to see the things I have seen
I wish it was all a horrible dream.
I've seen more that a child's eyes should see
But this is it, it's reality.
I wish I was in another place
So these things I wouldn't have to face.
I'm a Palestinian child it seems I don't have a choice
Please someone listen, I do have a voice.

Michelle Amani Darhali

The Price of War

Your country is at war. Your lives are torn apart.
What once was yours, only remains in your heart.
You have nothing left, no money, no home.
Your family have been taken, you are left on your own.
All that remain, are the clothes on your back.
And a few little memories, you chucked in a sack.
There's no food or shelter, there's nowhere to hide.
You'll do anything you can, just to stay alive.
So you start walking, you meet up with others.
Lonely dads, mothers, sisters and brothers.
They are all alone, they've lost everything too.
they have nothing left, just like you.
You all decide to walk, to another land.
They will have mercy on you, they will understand.
So you walk for weeks you are hungry and cold.
You have been joined with others, young and old.
Some are too weak, they die on the way.
There's nothing you can do, the others say.
So you keep on moving. Your heart filed with hope and fear.
It's not long to go now, the borders are near.
You can see in the distance, the bright shining lights.
You know when you get there, it will be alright.
But when you arrive, your joy turns to pain.
Your last few weeks have all been in vain.
You're refused entry, we can't take you no more.
They turn you away, and lock the door.
No kindness, no care, no compassion, no cover.
Is this how we end up treating each other?
The world has gone cold, full of heartache and grief.
We are all human, and all we want is peace.

Michelle Amani Darhali

A Child of War.

I used to live in such a happy place.
Where everyone had a smile on their face.
Me and my friends would play together.
I thought our smiles would last forever.
Then the rockets came landing, so close by.
Hold me tight mummy, in case we die.
When all was silent upon the ground.
I went out, to have a look around.
There was nothing left, no homes, no school.
Why do adults have to be so cruel?
I asked daddy why? What have we done?
He said, "it is not your fault my son."
"Believe me you've done nothing wrong,
You just have to be brave and carry on."
Then the soldiers came marching down the street.
The ground shook with the sound of their heavy feet.
They started firing, they were shooting so wild.
"Please don't hurt me, I'm just a child."
One looked at me with a cold-hearted grin.
But just like a robot, there was no heart in him.
Such innocent children being killed every day,
Our poor innocent lives just taken away.
Then the most beautiful of angels came right next to me.
With the most beautiful smiles you will ever see.
We are taking you to heaven
Where there's no more suffering or pain.
Where everyone has smiles on their faces again

Michelle Amani Darhali

A human Refugee

When you look at me
Tell me, what do you see.
Do you see a human being,
Or just another refugee.
I was once like you
I had a job and a home
A family and a car
But now I'm all on my own.
When the bombs came falling
And my house fell to the ground.
There was nothing left
For miles around.
I had a family abroad
Who would help me out.
So, my only choice was
To leave and get out.
My heart was broken
As I was leaving this place.
With an unknown future
That I had to face.
Now I have to beg others
For the food that I eat.
For the clothes on my back
And the shoes on my feet.
Do you ever stop to think
What would you do?
Because in this uncertain future
This could be you.

Michelle Amani Darhali

Whispers of Tomorrow

" Do you think the dawn will come?» she asked,
Her voice soft, almost lost in the hum of the restless sea.
I looked at her, this child of the earth,
Her eyes too young to hold such sorrow,
And I said, *"Yes, it will. It always does."*

"But the rubble still stands," she whispered.
"The walls don't remember what they were.
Do you think flowers can bloom where the soil is so tired?"
And I told her, *"Even tired soil cradles seeds.*
Give it time, and the flowers will come. They always do."

She stared at the cracked horizon,
Where the sun struggled to break through the gray,
And I saw her searching for colors
That only hope could paint.
"Will the laughter return?" she asked.

"Laughter hides in silence sometimes," I said.
"But it never leaves. It will rise again—
In the streets, in the fields, in your voice.
You'll see. Joy has a way of finding its way home."

Her hands traced the outline of a dream
She hadn't dared to speak aloud.
"Do you think we'll ever be whole again?" she said,
Her words trembling, fragile as a bird's wing.

"Not whole as before," I replied,
"For the scars will remain.
But even scars can shine under the right light.
And from those cracks, something stronger grows—
Something that can never be broken again."

She looked at me, eyes now steady.
"Do you really believe that?"
And I smiled, because believing was the only choice.
"Yes. I do. Because even the darkest night
Always carries whispers of tomorrow."

And as the sea sang its quiet hymn,
She nodded, just once,
Her small hands holding tightly to the promise of dawn.

Sidra Mobeen, Swindon, UK

Paradise

I walk around the chilly aisles, piped music playing, eyeing special offers,
I stand on the tarmac as the bell rings and children bubble out of classrooms,
I pit olives, chop fresh tomatoes and coriander, news in the background,
I put dirty clothes in the machine, soak up its reassuring churning,
I close my front door, the solid wood warm under my palm, almost breathing,
I am wrapped in the unwritten covenant
between us, daily life founded only on trust,
my sanity is sanitised. I can choose to turn the radio off.

There, the boom showers portions across the market, crimson runs in the gutters, pooling, sticky,
Elsewhere, the classroom is full of absences, walls pitted with dark cavities,
In a foreign place, a broken cup scoops up dirty water, raised to lips,
Not here, sweat bloomed clothes wear hungry ghosts, standing in line,
Far away, a broken doorframe creaks a lament, whilst something charred smoulders,
The promises are lost to dust, the dust sweeps through the potholed streets,
The journalist is twitchy, waiting for the link to go live, hoping someone cares
beyond the static.

Khadija Rouf

Pomegranate

Dedicated to the humanitarian work of Dr David Nott.

I.
The doctor did not see: power makes you sick. His roar sprayed blood on marble.

The shrapnel shrieks of wingless birds blistered bricks. Incised from pock holes, bitter fruit passes from mouth to mouth. Children will speak stones for generations. Yet, the sun still dares to rise, sliding across dust, casting small shadows - dark twins to rubble. The mosque gone. The blackened branches of the pomegranate witness strange windfalls,

fruits crushed into the dark, dry earth.

The faces of buildings are shorn off. Dolls houses reveal remnants of a life, covered

in the snow fall of ash. Dazed, Nadia sits on her sofa, staring out of a wall-less room

at her charred city. She takes sips of breath and weeps. Green gardens have crumpled

under brittle rain. Ancient olives are splintered. The sycamore, the tamarisk, the almond

cut down. For those who still live, there is hunger and thirst and fear. No-one knows when there could there be a moment for peace

Because there is no governance in war. Adam remembers he was a man, but

Hell is the distance of a trigger finger's squeeze. Dolls fall down. He dreams of rictus smiles,

the radium bones of a baby, with a bullet in its brain. There are no jinn: just his reflection

curved in a bullet, the relentless beat of taking aim. He sees it, running with bread in its arms. The bullet is swift but the wound is slow. The earth clots and days pass until Nadia slips out of fever, and melts into the underworld.

II.

In a parallel time, continuous like a singing river, there is peace.
In the sahn garden, seeds flame into aromatic trees, cornflowers,
mandrakes and damask roses. Food is waiting for guests – dishes of figs,
almonds, dates and olives. A breeze exhales blossom and birdsong and
the earth gives up petrochor. The fountain is a mosaic of water and sunlight,
illuminating minarets which are pinned to the skyline. The souks bustle.
Here, people are patient with small details, they make beautiful things.
Potters stain ceramics with cinnabar. Cooks carefully grind spices into bharat.
The doctor cups his palm, holds cumin seeds and chickpeas like a prize.

In a cloistered corner, Adam and Nadia kiss under a pomegranate tree.
He weaves myrtle and jasmine into her black hair. Her lips are butterfly wings,
feverish at his neck. He sees his reflection in her eyes, as their fingertips touch.
She places a pomegranate seed on his tongue and breathes,
'I am you'.

Khadija Rouf

(published in 'Just Words Too', 2017, by the Headington Writers)

The Twelve Days of Christmas In Gaza

On the first day of Christmas
My pension bought for me
A burned down olive tree.

On the second day of Christmas
My pension bought for me
Bullets and guns,
And a burned down olive tree.

On the third day of Christmas
My pension bought for me
Fear and dread,
Bullets and guns,
And a burned down olive tree.

On the fourth day of Christmas
My pension bought for me
Bunker busting bombs,
Fear and dread,
Bullets and guns,
And a burned down olive tree.

On the fifth day of Christmas
My pension bought for me
Weapons galore!
Bunker busting bombs,
Fear and dread,
Bullets and guns,
And a burned down olive tree.

On the sixth day of Christmas
My pension bought for me
Killer drones a-plenty,
Weapons galore!
Bunker busting bombs,
Fear and dread,
Bullets and guns,
And a burned down olive tree.

On the seventh day of Christmas
My pension bought for me
More Hellfire missiles,
Killer drones a-plenty,
Weapons galore!
Bunker busting bombs,
Fear and dread,
Bullets and guns,
And a burned down olive tree.

On the eighth day of Christmas
My pension bought for me
Fighter jet components,
More Hellfire missiles,
Killer drones a-plenty,
Weapons galore!
Bunker busting bombs,
Fear and dread,
Bullets and guns,
And a burned down olive tree.

On the ninth day of Christmas
My pension bought for me
F16 bombers,
Fighter jet components,
More Hellfire missiles,
Killer drones a-plenty,
Weapons galore!
Bunker busting bombs,
Fear and dread,
Bullets and guns,
And a burned down olive tree.

On the tenth day of Christmas
My pension bought for me
Missile launching hardware,
F16 bombers,
Fighter jet components,
More hellfire missiles,
Killer drones a-plenty,
Weapons galore!
Bunker busting bombs,
Fear and dread,
Bullets and guns,
And a burned down olive tree.

On the eleventh day of Christmas
My pension bought for me
Ammo loading systems,
Missile launching hardware,
F16 bombers,
Fighter jet components,
More hellfire missiles,

Killer drones a-plenty,
Weapons galore!
Bunker busting bombs,
Fear and dread,
Bullets and guns,
And a burned down olive tree.

On the twelfth day of Christmas
My pension bought for me
Weaponised quadcopters,
Ammo loading systems,
Missile launching hardware,
F16 bombers,
Fighter jet components,
More hellfire missiles,
Killer drones a-plenty,
Weapons galore!
Bunker busting bombs
Fear and dread,
Bullets and guns,
And a burned down olive tree.

Jane Samson

Adapted version of this carol read out at the Avon Pension Fund Committee meeting in Keynsham, UK

The Fall of Gaza

They are killing thousands of people without batting an eye
While the rest of the world stands idly by
In Gaza they mourn children blown up in their bed
Whilst by the rest of the world, barely a tear is shed.

Where else in the world could this injustice be done
To people who are trapped with nowhere to run
Within the tiny sliver of land on which they dwell
They are truly living through a tortured hell

With naked aggression the bombs keep falling
Killing babies and children, it's just appalling
Why do these innocent lives need to be lost
No objective can ever be worth this cost

But the power in this world is held by a select few
And they will never listen to neither me nor you
They have their own agendas, while disregarding the law
Continuing to justify murder by dressing it up as war

So, how many more people must die in vain
And how long can they continue to bear such pain
When everything they once loved or owned has gone
We must never forget them until justice is done.

Stella Mortazavi

Until

Until we stop taking and learn how to give
There will never be peace in this land where we live
Until we stop killing others because of their race
And stop judging people by the colour of their face

Until we stop preaching religion and let people decide
What they want to believe in, faith should come from inside
Until we stop fighting wars which we really don't need
What we spend on war, the whole world we could feed

Until we remove poverty and start helping the poor
And stop being so greedy, because less can be more
Until we live next to our neighbours without taking their lands
And realise that the fate of this world lies in all our hands

Until we can say that hate is truly a thing of the past
Only then can the peace we seek possibly last
Until we can look deep into our hearts and find
Love and respect for the whole of mankind

So, we need to start planting seeds of hope all around
Until true peace in this world is finally found
Because only then can we really begin to live
As we will have learned not to take, but to give.

Stella Mortazavi

www.ingramcontent.com/pod-product-compliance
Lightning Source LLC
LaVergne TN
LVHW011212080426
835508LV00007B/747